What Kind of Animal Is It?

# Reptiles of All Kinds

Kelley MacAulay and Bobbie Kalman

A Crabtree Crown Book

Crabtree Publishing

crabtreebooks.com

# Reptiles of All Kinds

**Editor-in-chief**
Bobbie Kalman

**Writing team**
Kelley MacAulay
Bobbie Kalman

**Substantive editor**
Kathryn Smithyman

**Editors**
Molly Aloian
Kristina Lundblad
Reagan Miller
Rebecca Sjonger

**Design**
Margaret Salter

**Consultant**
Patricia Loesche, Ph.D., Animal Behavior Program, Department of Psychology, University of Washington

**Junior consultant**
Thomas Brissenden

**Production manager**
Candice Campbell

**Images**
Kathy Kantor: page 21 (right);
All other images: Shutterstock.com, Corbis, Corel, Digital Stock, Digital Vision y Photodisc

**Crabtree Publishing**

crabtreebooks.com 800-387-7650



In Canada: We acknowledge the financial support of the Government of Canada through the Canada Book Fund for our publishing activities.

Printed in the U.S.A./CP032026

**Published in Canada**
**Crabtree Publishing**
616 Welland Ave.
St. Catharines,
Ontario L2M 5V6

**Published in the United States**
**Crabtree Publishing**
347 Fifth Ave.
Suite 1402-145
New York, NY 10016

Hardcover: 978-1-0398-7322-3
Paperback: 978-1-0398-7380-3
Ebook (pdf): 978-1-0398-7429-9
Epub: 978-1-0398-7478-7

**Library and Archives Canada Cataloguing in Publication**
Available at Library and Archives Canada

**Library of Congress Cataloging-in-Publication Data**
Available at the Library of Congress

# Contents

# Many kinds of reptiles

There are many kinds of **reptiles**! Some reptiles are big, and others are small. Reptiles belong to four groups. How many of these reptiles do you know?

*gavial*

*caiman*

*alligator*

*crocodile*

1. Crocodiles, alligators, caimans, and gavials make up one group of reptiles.

*tortoise*

2. Turtles and tortoises make up another group of reptiles.

*lizard*

*snake*

3. Snakes and lizards make up the largest group of reptiles.

*tuatara*

4. Tuataras make up their own group of reptiles.

# Reptiles have scales

All reptiles have skin made of **scales**.
Some reptiles have smooth scales.
Other reptiles have rough scales.
Scales protect a reptile's body.

*The Natal green snake has smooth scales.*

## More about scales

As reptiles grow, they lose their old scales and grow new scales. Losing scales is called **shedding**. Reptiles shed many times. Snakes shed all their scales in one big piece. Lizards shed their scales in smaller pieces. Lizards often eat the pieces!

*This lizard has rough scales all over its body.*

# Cold blood

Reptiles are **cold-blooded** animals. The body of a cold-blooded animal is the same temperature as the place where the animal lives. When the weather is cold, a reptile's body is cold. When the weather is warm, a reptile's body is warm. Most reptiles live in warm places.

*(left) The snake-necked turtle lives in Australia.*

*(above) This basilisk lizard lives in South America.*

## Staying healthy

Reptiles cannot stay healthy if their bodies are too hot or too cold. When reptiles are cold, they lie in the sun to get warm. When reptiles are too warm, they cool off in a shady spot. This snake was too hot. It has moved into the shade to cool off.

*This pink agama lizard is sitting in the sun to warm its body.*

# Reptile bodies

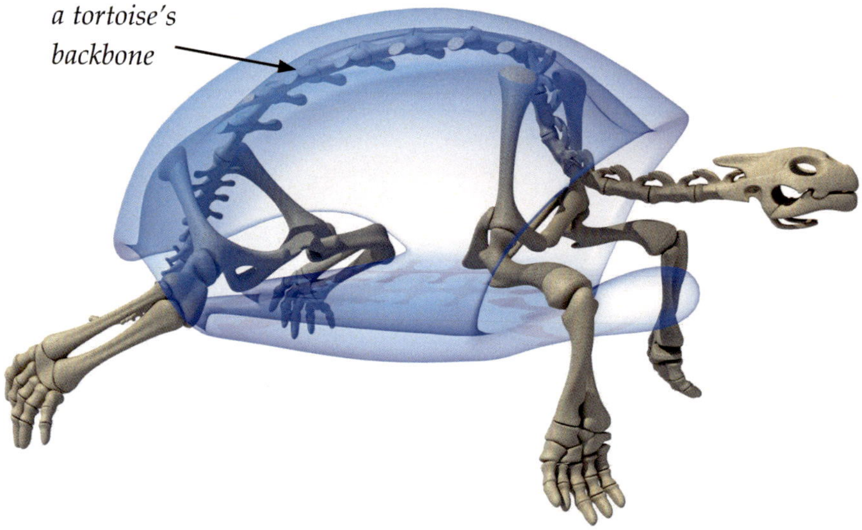


All reptiles have **backbones** inside their bodies. A backbone is a group of bones that run down the middle of an animal's back.

*A tortoise's backbone is attached to its shell.*

## How do reptiles move?

Most reptiles have legs. Reptiles with legs can walk, run, or swim. Snakes do not have legs, but some snakes can swim. On land, snakes move by **slithering**. To slither is to slide on the belly. Try slithering on your belly! Can you move like a snake?

*Crocodiles have short legs, but they can still run quickly!*

*Some snakes slither slowly. Others slither quickly.* *Turn to page 21 to learn about the different ways snakes move.*

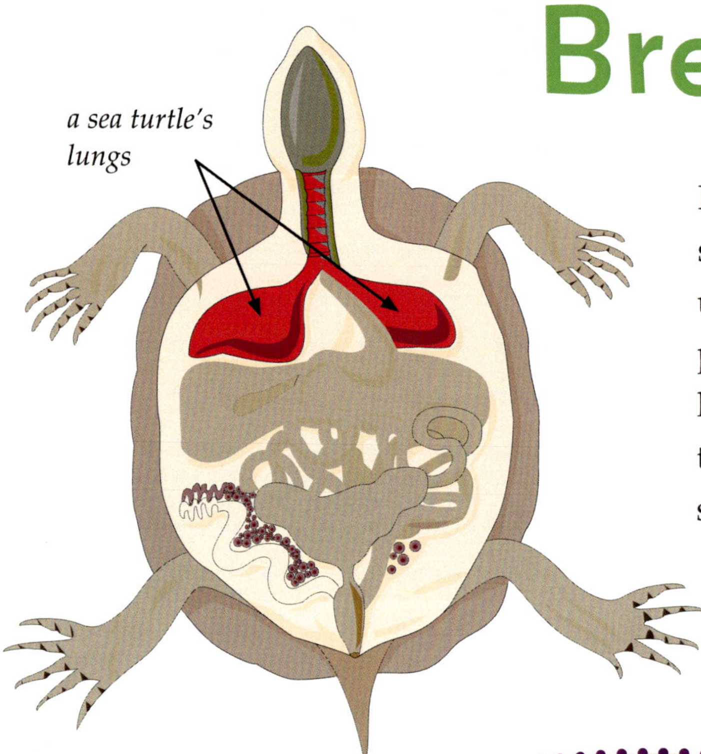


# Breathing air

Reptiles must breathe air to stay alive. They breathe air using **lungs**. Lungs are body parts that take in air. They also let out air. Most reptiles have two lungs, but many types of snakes have only one lung.

*Sidewinder snakes have only one lung.*

## Living in water

Some reptiles live in water. Reptiles that live in water still need to breathe air. They swim up to the top of the water to breathe.

*Alligators live in water and on land. When they come up for air, only their eyes and nostrils show above the water.*

*This sea snake lives in water. It needs to breathe air every fifteen minutes. To breathe, a sea snake lifts its head above the water.*

# Reptile babies

Most reptile babies hatch from eggs. Their mothers lay the eggs on land. Some reptiles lay hard eggs. Other reptiles lay soft eggs. After hatching, baby reptiles look just like small adult reptiles!

### Breaking through

Each baby reptile has an **egg tooth**. An egg tooth is a hard tooth on a baby's face. The baby uses its egg tooth to break through its egg. The egg tooth falls off after the baby is out of its egg.

*Skinks are lizards. Some kinds of skinks are born live.*

## Born live

A few types of reptiles do not hatch from eggs. They are **born live**. Reptiles that are born live are not inside eggs when they come out of their mothers' bodies.

## On their own

Most reptile mothers do not take care of their babies. The baby reptiles must take care of themselves.

*Many types of rattlesnakes are born live.*

# Reptile habitats

A **habitat** is the natural place where an animal lives. Different reptiles live in different habitats. Most reptiles live in warm habitats, such as deserts. Other reptiles live in habitats such as forests and swamps.

*Boa snakes live in forests. They often hang over tree branches.*

*The chuckwalla lizard lives in rocky deserts.*

*Alligators, crocodiles, and gavials live near water. Many live in swamps. The reptile in the picture above is a gavial. It lives in swamps in a country called India.*

## A long sleep

Some reptiles live in places that have cold winters. Reptiles that live in these habitats must **hibernate**. To hibernate means to sleep through winter. Garter snakes hibernate in groups. Staying together keeps the snakes warm.

*Iguanas are lizards. They are herbivores. This iguana is eating a cactus.*

# Finding Food

Different reptiles eat different foods. Some reptiles are **herbivores**. Herbivores are animals that eat plants.

## Eating other animals

Most reptiles are **carnivores**. Carnivores eat other animals. The animals that they eat are called **prey**. Some reptiles are **omnivores**. Omnivores eat plants, but they also eat other animals.

*The gila monster is also a lizard. It is a carnivore. It is eating eggs. It also eats mice.*

*Chameleons are lizards. They are omnivores. They eat plants and many kinds of insects.*

*A Komodo dragon is a lizard. It is a carnivore. It hunts large animals such as goats.*

## Did you know?

Did you know that snakes can open their jaws wider than any other animal can? Big snakes can open their jaws wide enough to swallow pigs! This snake is eating a frog.

# Slithering snakes

Some snakes make **venom** in their bodies. Venom is poison. Snakes use their venom to kill prey. The cobra snake above makes venom in its body. Cobra snakes sometimes use their venom to kill other snakes! Cobras eat the snakes they kill.

## Poisonous fangs

Snakes that make venom have two **fangs**. Fangs are sharp teeth. Most fangs have **grooves**. When a snake bites, its venom slides down the grooves in its fangs. The venom goes into a prey's body.

*Rattlesnakes have rattles on the ends of their tails. The snakes shake their rattles when they feel scared. The sound warns other animals to stay away!*

*Snakes have clear eyelids that cover their eyes. Eyelids keep dirt out of a snake's eyes.*

## Wiggling around

Different snakes slither in different ways. Here are some ways that snakes move.

*To move forward, some snakes curl up their bodies and then stretch them out.*

*To move sideways, some snakes push their bodies from side to side.*

*When some snakes move, their bodies look like waves.*

# A lot of lizards!

Most lizards have small bodies with short legs. Many lizards have tails that can be pulled off. When a carnivore grabs a lizard's tail, the lizard pulls its body away. Its tail comes off, and the lizard runs away. The lizard's tail soon grows back.

*This lizard can stand up and run on its back legs!*

*Komodo dragons are the biggest lizards in the world. Some are over nine feet (2.7 m) long! These lizards are longer than most cars!*

## Changing colors

Chameleons are famous lizards! They can change their skin color to match the colors around them.

*A chameleon can move each of its eyes in a different direction. One eye watches for prey. The other eye watches for danger.*

*A chameleon wraps its strong tail around a tree branch to hold on.*

# Reptiles with shells

Turtles and tortoises are different in some ways. Turtles have thin shells. They live mainly in water. Many live in ponds, lakes, and streams. Tortoises have thick, strong shells. They live on land. Many tortoises live in deserts.

*Turtles and tortoises walk slowly because their shells are heavy.*

*When a turtle or tortoise is afraid, it pulls its body into its shell for protection.*

## Sea turtles

Sea turtles live in oceans. They have **flippers** that help them swim. Their smooth bodies also help them swim. Sea turtles leave the water only to lay eggs.

sea turtle eggs

flipper

### Soft shells

Some types of turtles have soft shells. Their shells are made of thick skin. The shells can be cut easily. Soft shells do not protect turtles as well as hard shells do.

# Sharp teeth!

Crocodiles, alligators, caimans, and gavials live in rivers and swamps. They have long heads. Their mouths are filled with sharp teeth. These reptiles also have heavy bodies and strong tails. They use their strong tails for swimming.

*Gavials have more than 50 teeth. Their teeth help them catch fish. Fish is their main food.*

## Which is which?

Alligators, caimans, and crocodiles look alike, but their heads have different shapes. Learn how to tell them apart!

*alligator*

*An alligator's head is short. It is shaped like the letter "U." When an alligator's mouth is closed, few of its teeth show.*

*caiman*

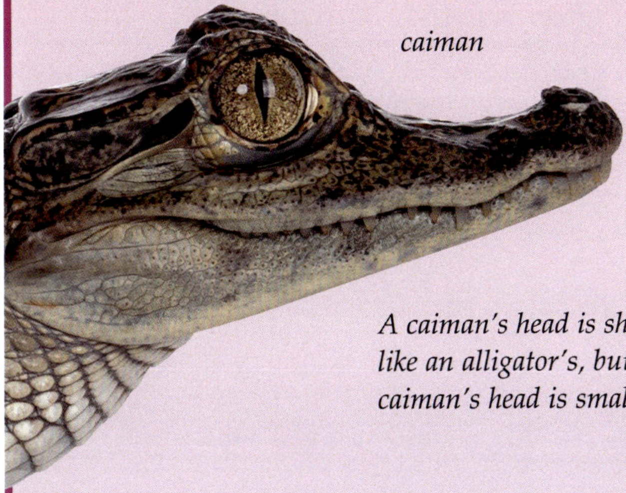

*A caiman's head is shaped like an alligator's, but the caiman's head is smaller.*

*crocodile*

*A crocodile's head is long. It is shaped like the letter "V." When the crocodile has its mouth closed, its long teeth stick out.*

*gavial*

*The gavial has a long and narrow head. Its small teeth are hard to see.*

# Tuataras

Tuataras lived on Earth even before the dinosaurs lived here! A long time ago, there were other reptiles in the tuatara group. The other reptiles are now **extinct**. Extinct animals no longer live anywhere on Earth.

*Most tuataras live to be 60 years old! Tuataras live only on some small islands near New Zealand.*

## Liking the cold

Most reptiles like warm weather, but tuataras prefer colder weather. Tuataras like to sleep during the days, when it is hot. They hunt for food during the nights, when it is cool. Tuataras eat bird eggs, small animals, and many kinds of insects.

*Tuataras eat spiders. They also eat beetles and other insects.*

*A tuatara has three eyes! Its third eye is under the skin between its other two eyes. A tuatara can see colors with its third eye, but it cannot see shapes.*

# Matching reptiles

In this book, you have learned that reptiles belong to four different groups. Can you remember which reptiles belong to which groups? Here is a fun way to test how much you remember. Play the Reptile Memory Game! Ask your family and friends to read this book so they can play the game with you!

*Are tortoises and lizards in the same group of reptiles?*

## How to make the game

1. Cut up some paper to make 30 square cards.
2. Draw a different reptile on each card. Make sure you have at least two reptiles from each group!
3. Write the name of the reptile above each drawing.

## How to play

1. Spread out the cards face-down on the floor.
2. Have each player take a turn flipping over two cards.
3. If the reptiles on the cards are from the same group, the player has a match. The player keeps the two matching cards.
4. If the reptiles are from different groups, ask the player to flip the cards back over. Try to remember the reptiles on the cards and where the cards are!
5. The person holding the most matching cards at the end of the game is the winner!

*Before you make the cards, look at pages 4 and 5 to make sure you know your reptile groups. Then draw as many reptiles as you can. Use this book to help you remember! Don't forget to draw the tuatara twice!*

# Words to know and Index

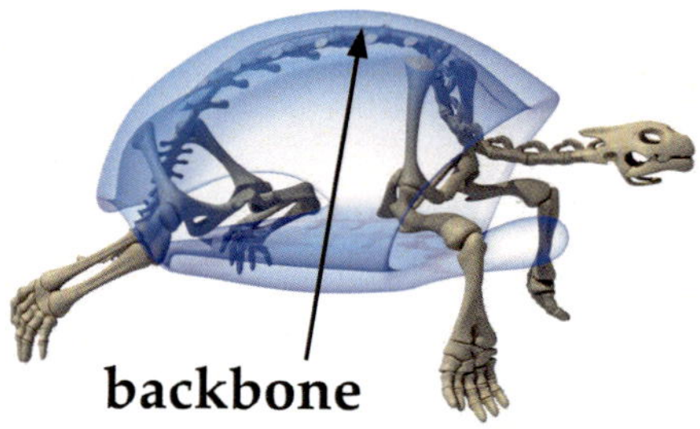